The
Constellations

by Peggy J. Parks

KIDHAVEN PRESS

An imprint of Thomson Gale, a part of The Thomson Corporation

THOMSON

GALE

Detroit • New York • San Francisco • San Diego • New Haven, Conn. • Waterville, Maine • London • Munich

LIBRARY OF CONGRESS CATALOGING-IN-PUBLICATION DATA

Parks, Peggy J., 1951–
  The constellations / by Peggy J. Parks.
    p. cm. — (The KidHaven science library)
  Includes bibliographical references and index.
  ISBN 0-7377-3054-4 (lib. bdg. : alk. paper)
  1. Constellations—Juvenile literature. I. Title. II. Series.
  QB802.P29 2005
  523.8—dc22
                                                        2005013831

Printed in the United States of America

Contents

Chapter 1

Pictures in the Sky

When the night is clear, thousands of stars are visible in the sky. They shine and twinkle like diamonds scattered across black velvet. Humans have been fascinated with stars for thousands of years, perhaps even as long as life has existed on Earth. But in ancient times, it was difficult for people to tell the stars apart or to find them again when they moved. So, they connected the stars with imaginary lines to form pictures. The late scientist and author Isaac Asimov described this:

> It would be simple to divide them up as squares, triangles, crosses, and other shapes, but that's not distinctive enough, and besides it doesn't satisfy human beings, who are, to a surprising degree, poets and artists at heart. Therefore, they chose combinations of stars that looked (if you have a terrific imagination) like bears, or hunters, or eagles, or scorpions. These are now called "**constellations**" from Latin words meaning "with stars."[1]

Sky Diamonds

Scientists who study the skies are known as **astronomers**. They have identified a total of 88 constellations, which are grouped into eight families. Some of these constellations are tiny, with just a few stars, while others are enormous.

The stars within constellations look like pinpricks of light in the sky. However, they are actually massive and much larger than the Earth. Stars appear to be small because they are trillions of miles away. They are so far from the Earth that their distance is measured in **light-years**, rather than miles or kilometers. A light-year is based on the speed of

This seventeenth-century illustration shows the stars that form Ursa Major, one of the most recognizable constellations in the nighttime sky.

This bright cluster made up of hundreds of thousands of stars is found in the constellation Centaurus.

light. One light-year equals nearly 6 trillion miles (9.6 trillion km).

Stars are made of glowing balls of hot gases, mostly hydrogen and helium. They vary in color depending on how hot they are. For example, stars that are blue or white are the hottest. The high temperature causes the stars to burn their fuel more quickly than cooler stars. Astronomers believe the hottest stars last from 10,000 to 100,000 years before they run out of fuel. The next hottest are yellow stars, which live for about 10 billion years. Earth's sun is an example of a yellow star. It is about 5 billion years old and will live about 5 billion more years. The smallest and coolest stars are red dwarfs. These stars burn their fuel very slowly, so they live a very long time. Some red dwarfs live for trillions of years.

One example of a red dwarf is Proxima Centauri. It is considered a small star, but it is still nearly five times the size of the Earth. Proxima Centauri is part of a constellation called Centaurus. The ancient Greeks named Centaurus after the centaur, an imaginary beast that was half man and half horse. To modern stargazers, Centaurus does not look much like a centaur. But the people of ancient Greece were convinced it was a wise and kind centaur known as Chiron. They believed Chiron was raised to the sky after being accidentally struck by a poisoned arrow.

From Sea Serpents to Winged Horses

Centaurus and other constellations are not always visible, nor can they be seen everywhere in the world. Science writer Chris Sasaki explains: "The sky puts on a slightly different show for you every night. We see some stars in winter. Others we see on summer nights. We also see different stars, depending on where we are on Earth."[2] Centaurus can be seen best during autumn in the Southern Hemisphere, including Africa, Australia, South America, and Antarctica.

Another southern constellation is Hydra. It is the largest and longest constellation in the sky. The ancient Greeks named Hydra after an imaginary water serpent with many heads. It was believed to

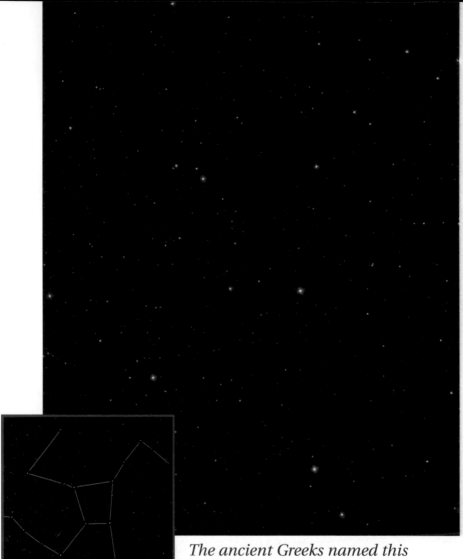

The ancient Greeks named this constellation Hercules because they thought it looked like their mythological hero swinging a club.

be a fierce monster that killed people with its poisonous breath. The Greek hero, Hercules, tried to slay Hydra. Every time he cut off one of its heads, however, others would grow back in its place. Finally, Hercules succeeded in killing the beast with his club. Yet even though Hydra had been fierce and deadly, the Greeks respected its great power and gave it a place among the stars.

In honor of the hero who slayed Hydra, there is a constellation called Hercules. It is most visible in the Northern Hemisphere and looks like a man swinging a club. Hercules is a large constellation, but it is not very bright because it is so far away. When Hercules can be seen, a faint, hazy, starlike object is visible on its head. This is actually a cluster of many thousands of stars known as the Great Cluster of Hercules.

Another northern constellation is Pegasus. The ancient Greeks named it after a great winged horse. According to Greek legend, Pegasus's mother was killed. Afterward, the orphaned horse flew free and wild through the sky. Eventually, a horse master tamed Pegasus and fitted him with a fine, golden bridle. Together, the horse and rider swooped down and killed a fire-breathing monster named Chimera. But Pegasus was not happy because he wanted to fly on his own. So, he tossed his rider and flew off to the heavens, where he was given a very important job. It was his responsibility to carry lightning bolts for Zeus, the king of the gods.

Constellations and Asterisms

Not far from Pegasus is a small constellation called Delphinius. It was named after a dolphin, the creature it resembles. According to one ancient Greek legend, a sea god sent Delphinius on a mission. The dolphin was to find a sea nymph named Amphitrite and marry her. He completed his mission and was rewarded with a place in the heavens.

Great Bear is another constellation that resembles the creature for which it is named. Officially called Ursa Major, it is a famous constellation. That is because a star formation known as the Big Dipper is inside it. The Big Dipper looks very much like a giant ladle. Its bowl is sitting on the bear's shoulder like a saddle, while the tip of the handle forms

Delphinius's distinct dolphin shape makes it easily recognizable in the nighttime sky.

the bear's nose. Since it appears inside a constellation, the Big Dipper is a type of star pattern known as an **asterism**. It is made up of seven stars: three that form the handle, and four that form the bowl.

The two brightest stars in the Big Dipper's bowl point directly toward Polaris. This star is the most famous star in the world and is also called the North Star or Pole Star. Polaris is not the brightest or biggest star in the sky, but it has guided people for centuries. That is because it appears directly over the North Pole. Of all the stars, Polaris is the only one that does not move. It always sits in the north, always in the same spot, while other stars move around it. Author H.A. Rey explains this: "Imagine a giant umbrella, with the Pole Star as its center and yourself at the handle. On the umbrella are the Big Dipper and [the constellation] Cassiopeia. You see them go around the Pole Star as the umbrella slowly turns. We know of course that the sky does not really turn but that it is the earth which does the turning. The effect, however, is the same."[3] Polaris is part of another asterism called the Little Dipper, which is found inside the constellation Ursa Minor.

Throughout history, humans have been fascinated with stars. In ancient times, people formed imaginary pictures and created legends to explain them. Those star pictures came to be known as constellations. The star watchers of today find them every bit as fascinating as the people who lived thousands of years ago.

Chapter 2

Mapping the Heavens

In the early 1600s, an Italian scientist named Galileo Galilei heard of a wondrous device that was invented in the Netherlands. It featured a tube with glass lenses at opposite ends and was used to make distant objects appear closer. Although Galileo had not actually seen it for himself, he became intrigued. He was a devout observer of the skies, and he believed such an instrument could help him study the stars and planets. In 1609, Galileo designed and built a sky-watching device of his own. It resembled a small pair of binoculars, and it would later become known as the telescope.

Galileo had not invented the telescope, but he was the first to use one for observing the skies. Although his telescope was small and the images were somewhat fuzzy, Galileo could see stars and constellations closer than anyone had ever seen them before.

Early Astronomers

Yet even without telescopes, people had been observing the skies for thousands of years before Galileo. Some early astronomers drew detailed charts and maps that showed the constellations. One was a Greek named Claudius Ptolemaeus, more commonly known as Ptolemy. In the 2nd century A.D., Ptolemy recorded more than a thousand stars. He grouped them into 48 constellations and recorded his findings in a book called *Almagest*. The book contained the first known star charts.

Ptolemy's work was considered important, but it contained several major flaws. For one thing, he

In this painting, Galileo Galilei teaches the English poet John Milton how to use a telescope to study the stars.

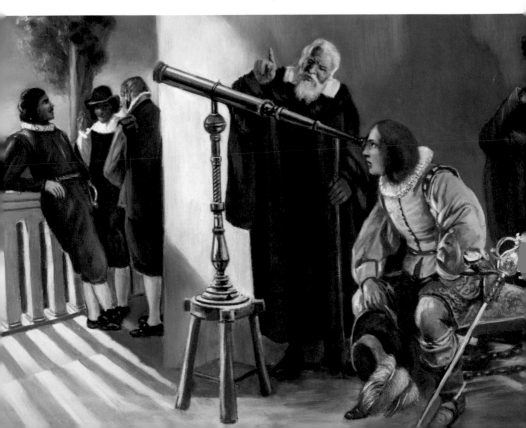

Earth — Venus
Mars — Neptune
Pluto — Mercury
Saturn — Uranus
Sun —
Jupiter

identified only northern constellations. Ptolemy lived in Egypt, and he was not able to see the southernmost constellations. So, that area of his chart showed a large void where there appeared to be no stars at all. Also, he believed in a **geocentric system**, meaning that the Earth was the center of the universe. Ptolemy was convinced that the Earth remained still while the stars, Sun, and planets all rotated around it. *Almagest* reflected this geocentric theory.

Ptolemy's beliefs were widely accepted among scientists. They were also embraced by the Roman Catholic Church, which believed the geocentric system to be consistent with the *Bible's* teachings. Anyone of the Catholic faith who disagreed could be severely punished or even killed. Because of the

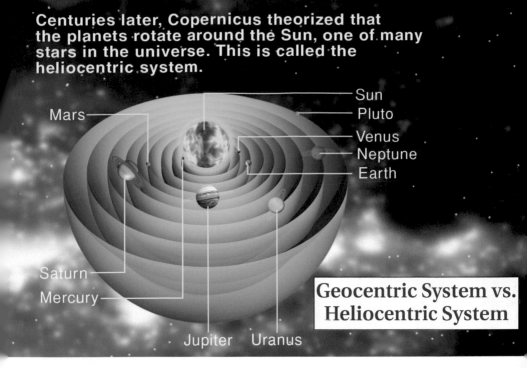

Centuries later, Copernicus theorized that the planets rotate around the Sun, one of many stars in the universe. This is called the heliocentric system.

Sun
Pluto
Venus
Neptune
Earth

Mars

Saturn
Mercury

Jupiter   Uranus

Geocentric System vs. Heliocentric System

risk, anyone who disagreed with Ptolemy did not dare to speak out.

Challenging Accepted Theories

Centuries passed before Ptolemy's geocentric theory was challenged. Finally, an amateur Polish astronomer named Nicolaus Copernicus made his own theories public. After studying the stars and planets for many years, he concluded that the geocentric system was wrong. He believed (correctly) that the Sun was the center of the universe and that all planets and stars moved around it. Copernicus wrote about his beliefs in a book entitled *On the Revolution of the Celestial Spheres*.

In the sixteenth century, Polish astronomer Nicolaus Copernicus developed a sun-centered theory of the universe.

Several decades later, a Danish astronomer named Tycho Brahe became aware of Copernicus's work. Tycho (as he was known) was curious about the skies and began his own observations. He founded an observatory on an island between Denmark and Sweden. It was called Uranienborg, which meant "fortress of the heavens." Over the following years, Tycho spent his nights studying the constellations and the planets. In the process, he made precise, comprehensive measurements of more than 700 stars. Not all of his conclusions were correct, though. For example, he believed that all planets except the Earth revolved around the Sun. The Earth, he thought, remained stationary while the Sun and other planets orbited it. However, in spite of this error, Tycho was admired for his many contributions to the field of astronomy.

An Elaborate Star Map

Yet neither Tycho nor any of the other astronomers who had charted the skies were aware of constellations in the far Southern Hemisphere. Then in the 1500s, Dutch explorers traveled to lands south of the equator. When they returned home, they told of what they had observed during their journey. They described the oceans, the lands, and the people. They also told of the southern skies where there were constellations they had never seen before.

In 1603, a German lawyer named Johann Bayer included the southern constellations in a publication called *Uranometria.* It was the world's first sky **atlas**, or collection of highly detailed star maps for the entire planet. *Uranometria* contained 51 different star maps, all of which were hand engraved on copper plates. Forty-eight of them showed the northern constellations that had been recorded by Ptolemy about fifteen hundred years before. The 49th map in Bayer's atlas showed twelve southern constellations. Many of these had been named after

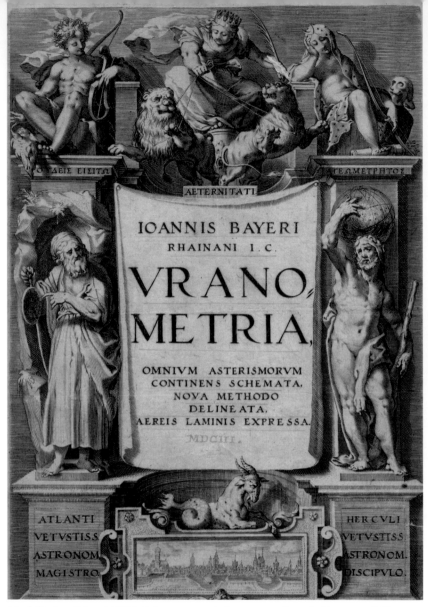

Published in 1603, Uranometria *contained the world's first maps of the constellations.*

birds, such as Tucana (toucan), Apus (bird of paradise), and Grus (crane or stork). The last 2 maps were overviews of constellations in both hemispheres. All in all, more than 1,200 stars were featured in *Uranometria.*

The Constellations of the Zodiac

One of the constellation families included in *Uranometria* was known as the **zodiac**. It had been discovered thousands of years before Bayer's time, although no one knows for sure exactly when. Some historians say the zodiac was first sighted by people in ancient Mesopotamia, which is now Iraq. However, no written record was published until the 3rd century B.C. A Greek poet named Aratus wrote a poem in 270 B.C. called *Phaenomena*. In the poem, he described 45 constellations, including those of the zodiac family.

A beautifully illustrated diagram from the eighteenth century shows the twelve constellations of the zodiac.

Ancient sky watchers were fascinated with the zodiac. The constellations formed a continuous band of twelve star patterns that stretched all the way across the sky. People watched the activity of these celestial bodies as the Sun and planets seemed to travel along the band. Each time the Moon circled the entire sky, the Sun moved over one constellation. Astronomer Von Del Chamberlain describes this:

Imagine watching the movements of the solar system from the Sun. Viewed from that high bright station we would see the entire fleet of planets, including Earth, move around us

This computer illustration shows how the stars in the zodiac constellation Scorpius form the scorpion's body.

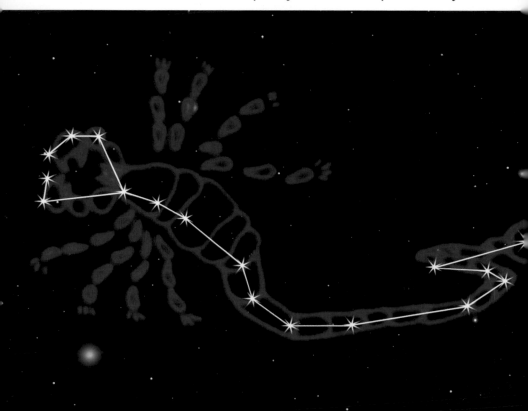

through the zodiac. Earth would trace a line we call the **ecliptic** and the other planets would trace paths nearly coinciding with the ecliptic. . . . From Earth we look out and see a changing relationship between the Sun by day and stars of the zodiac by night . . . the Sun appears to be moving through the zodiac. This is, of course, merely a reflection of our own orbital motion around the Sun.[4]

The constellations in the zodiac were given Greek names. Some were named after animals or mythical creatures, while others were either human or part human. There was a ram named Aries, a lion named Leo, and a creature that was half goat and half fish named Capricorn. Another such creature was Taurus, which was half man and half bull. Pisces was a fish, Cancer was a crab, and Scorpius was a poisonous insect known as a scorpion. Aquarius, Sagittarius, and Virgo represented people, as did Gemini, the twins. The twelfth constellation, Libra, was neither animal nor human; it represented a scale used for weighing objects.

Today's astronomers have much more knowledge about the constellations than those who lived thousands of years ago. Yet the work of the ancient star watchers was very important. They studied the stars, recorded what they saw, and left valuable information that helped future astronomers better understand the skies.

Chapter 3

Guided by the Stars

Whether they are amateur sky watchers or professional astronomers, people find constellations to be fascinating. Night after night, they gaze at the sky and admire the intricate patterns of stars. Some may imagine they can see the mythical creatures envisioned by the ancient Greeks. Others may stare at the stars and see constellations in a way that no one has ever seen them before.

Navigation by the Stars

But in ancient times, people watched the skies for more than just enjoyment. They depended on stars to guide them when sailing the ocean. For example, the people of Phoenicia (modern-day Lebanon and Syria) used the stars as navigational tools. Most explorers could only travel through the ocean in the daytime because they relied on landmarks to find their way. But the Phoenicians used the stars, and they were the first to be able to sail at night.

They knew that the North Star was inside Ursa Minor and that it appeared directly over the North Pole. By finding the constellation in the sky, they could tell which direction their ships were heading. Ursa Minor was so important to the Phoenicians that they often called it Doube, which meant "guide."

The Importance of the Dog Star

The ancient Egyptians also looked to the night skies for guidance. They kept a close watch on Sirius, the brightest star in the sky. Sirius was part of the constellation Canis Major (meaning "Greater Dog") and was often called the Dog Star. Since the Egyptian climate did not change much throughout the year, it was difficult for people to tell what season it was. They learned to do this by watching how

This artwork shows how to locate the bright Pole star, or Polaris, between Ursa Major on the left and Cassiopeia on the right.

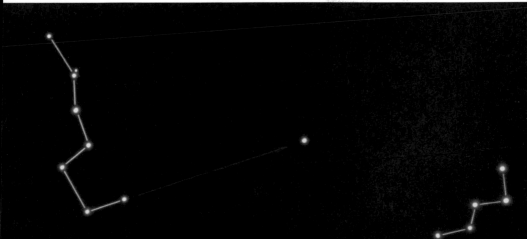

Part of the constellation Canis Major, the bright, blue-white star Sirius is the brightest star in the sky.

Sirius moved through the sky. They depended on the star so much that they developed their calendar based on its behavior. Farmers relied on Sirius for knowing when to plant their crops.

The ancient Egyptians also observed that Sirius's cycles coincided with the rise and fall of the Nile River. In mid-June, when the star was first visible in the sky, torrential rains would fall in the Ethiopian highlands. This caused the Nile to overflow, sweeping floodwaters through the Nile Valley. Because Egypt often went years without rain, the Egyptians welcomed the sight of Sirius. They knew that when it appeared the annual flood was on its way, and they captured the water in canals and basins. They could tell when the floodwaters were about to recede because Sirius moved higher in the sky.

Because of what the Nile meant to the Egyptians, they worshipped Sirius. They even constructed their temples so light from the star could shine in their inner altars. And since the Dog Star glowed so brightly, they believed it was responsible for the scorching summer temperatures. Although this belief was not correct, it led to the common phrase "dog days of summer."

Star Gazing and Astrology

People no longer need to rely on the stars to find out what month it is—but many still depend on the skies for guidance. These people believe **astrology**, which is the study of how earthly events are influenced by the Sun, Moon, planets, and stars. Astrologers (people who specialize in astrology) say that these celestial bodies can affect people's personalities as well as what happens to them in the future. People turn to astrology for advice on planning for the future, making important decisions, and sometimes even whether to get out of bed in the morning!

Astrologers make their predictions based on how celestial bodies interact with each other. They create charts called **horoscopes**, which are illustrated in a circle. The charts resemble drawings of the zodiac constellations because they are shown as a band around the ecliptic. Also, horoscope charts are divided into twelve individual parts, similar to the twelve zodiac constellations. However, on horoscope charts the parts are known as the twelve signs of the zodiac. These include Aries, Taurus, Gemini, Cancer, Leo, Virgo, Libra, Scorpio, Sagittarius, Capricorn, Aquarius, and Pisces. Because the Sun travels through each zodiac constellation at a particular time, signs of the zodiac are often called sun signs.

Astrology in some form has been practiced for thousands of years, but printed horoscopes have only existed since 1930. That was when the first horoscope appeared in a British newspaper called the *Sunday Express*. After that, the popularity of astrology began to grow.

Zodiac Planting

One way people use astrology is to help them decide when to plant gardens and crops. For example, those who practice **biodynamic gardening** believe that the movements of the Moon, planets, and stars can influence the growth and development of all plants. In an article called "Planting by the Stars," Teresa Coughlin writes: "At first glance the idea that the stars affect our garden seems quite crazy . . . [but] judging by the number of horoscopes in newspapers and magazines, it seems that many people accept that the movement of heavenly bodies can affect their lives. So why not . . . plants?"[5]

Coughlin cites experiments in Germany that were designed to show a connection between plant growth and the movement of celestial bodies. A woman named Maria Thun planted one plot of radishes every day during a growing season. She found the plots that produced the biggest roots were those she planted when the Moon was passing through the constellations of Virgo, Capricorn, or Taurus. So, she performed experiments with other root crops such as carrots and onions. These,

A zodiac wheel illustrates the relationship between the twelve signs of the zodiac and the Sun.

too, flourished during the same period of time. In addition, the radishes Thun planted when the Moon was in Scorpius, Cancer, or Pisces, were much leafier than those planted during other times. She experimented with leafy plants such as lettuce, spinach, and parsley, and those plants flourished as well.

Afterward, Thun began publishing a yearly calendar for people interested in biodynamic gardening. Entitled *Working with the Stars,* it indicated the best days and times for planting flowers and vegetables. Today, the calendar is called *Stella Natura 2005.* It offers gardeners advice about fighting insects, planting, and fertilizing based solely on the behavior of the celestial bodies.

Star-Studded Decisions

While some people rely on astrology for gardening advice, others use it to make major decisions. One of them is Michael Anderson, who owns an online financial company. Before starting his firm in 2003,

A postcard from the early twentieth century lists the supposed characteristics of a woman born under the sign of Scorpio.

If you are a girlie and born in OCT.

You'll be very beautiful. You will have a perfect complexion of the drug-store variety and you'll coh a rich hubby,

Anderson consulted with his astrologer, Madeline Gerwick-Brodeur. She owns a company called Polaris Business Guides. After studying the positions of the stars and planets, Gerwick-Brodeur recommended a specific time and date that Anderson should sign his legal papers. This, she told him, would ensure a more profitable future. The astrologer is convinced that by understanding planetary cycles, companies can be more successful.

People who do not have their own astrologer can seek advice from *The Old Farmer's Almanac* Web site. In the "Astrology and the Signs" forum, participants exchange ideas about the best time to get married, have a baby, get a haircut, mow their lawn, or clip a horse's tail. One person asked about the best day to have 22 teeth pulled. Another wanted to know when he should go to the hospital to have surgery on his knee.

Throughout history, people have looked to the stars for guidance. Those who lived in ancient times used them as navigational tools or as a way of determining the season. Today, some people rely on stars to help them make decisions about everything from gardening to investing money. They may have different reasons for watching the skies, but doing so is just as important to them as it was to people thousands of years ago.

Star Exploration

When modern astronomers use the word *constellations*, they are referring to particular regions of the sky. In the same way that the Earth is divided into countries, the sky is divided into constellations. This sort of system makes it easier to locate and study specific stars.

Astronomy Challenges

Today's astronomers can study the stars at a very close range by using telescopes that are sophisticated and powerful. As a result, they can see things that ancient sky watchers could never have imagined. Yet even astronomers using the most powerful telescopes can find it difficult to see stars clearly because of interference from Earth's atmosphere. It surrounds the planet like a protective blanket and is more than 18 miles (30km) thick. The National Aeronautics and Space Administration (NASA) explains:

The next time you gaze up at the night sky, you're likely to spot a twinkling star. But is it really twinkling? What looks like a twinkling star to our eyes is actually steady starlight that has been distorted, or bent, by the Earth's atmosphere. The visual effect of this distortion is like looking at an object through a glass of water. Telescopes here on the ground—which also must peer through Earth's atmosphere—are equally vulnerable to our atmosphere's visual tricks.[6]

This time-lapse image taken with a powerful telescope shows how stars appear to move in the sky.

The Hubble Space Telescope links up with the space shuttle Discovery *for repairs in 1999.*

Observing Space from Space

Scientists solved this problem by developing a new kind of telescope that would operate from space. In April 1990, the space shuttle *Discovery* launched the **Hubble Space Telescope**. It took up residence about 380 miles (612km) above the Earth, and it continues to orbit the planet today. The Hubble is as big as a large school bus and weighs 24,500 pounds (11,110kg)—as heavy as two full-grown elephants! It is fitted with sophisticated cameras and other instruments such as **spectrometers**. These allow astronomers to estimate a star's temperature and age by examining its color.

The Hubble can observe the light from celestial bodies before that light is distorted. As a result, the view is much sharper than that from even the largest telescope on the ground. As it travels along its orbit, it continuously transmits data back to Earth. Each week the Hubble sends about 120 gigabytes of data and photos to the Space Telescope Science Institute in Baltimore. That is enough data to fill books lining shelves that stretch 3,600 feet (1,097m) long.

During the years that the Hubble has been in space, it has taken more than 700,000 photographs. Astronomers have observed stars that were dying and others that were just being born. The new stars formed inside giant gas and dust clouds known as **nebulae**. Two Hubble photographs showed nebulae inside the constellation Orion. One of them was an eerie photograph that revealed a tall, billowing tower of gas and dust called the Eagle Nebula. Even though the nebula is 6,500 light-years away, astronomers actually watched clusters of new stars being created inside it. From that, they gained valuable knowledge about the process of star formation, which begins when gravity causes the gas clouds to collapse.

The Hubble also provides astronomers with photographs of distant **galaxies**. These are massive systems of stars that are held together by gravity. The Earth's galaxy (the **Milky Way**) is just one of billions of galaxies in the universe. One stunning Hubble photograph was of the Whirlpool Galaxy, which is more than 30 million light-years from Earth. NASA describes the galaxy as majestic, comparing it to a grand spiral staircase sweeping through space. The Whirlpool Galaxy has graceful, winding arms that fascinate astronomers.

Earth's Most Powerful Telescopes

Since the Hubble was launched in 1990, powerful ground-based telescopes have continued to be developed. The world's largest astronomy station, the W.M. Keck Observatory, is located in Hawaii. It is perched atop Mauna Kea, a dormant volcano that is 14,000 feet (4,267m) high. At that height, the atmosphere is thinner and does not interfere as

A 2001 image taken by the Hubble Space Telescope provides a detailed look at the distant Whirlpool galaxy.

much as at ground level. Still, it can create visibility problems at even the best observatories. To compensate, scientists have developed technology that can cancel the distortion caused by the atmosphere. The result is sharp, clear images of the sky.

The Keck Observatory has massive twin telescopes called the Keck Telescopes. They are the largest and most powerful ground telescopes in the world. Each stands eight stories tall and weighs 300 tons (272 metric tons). Like all telescopes, the Keck Telescopes have **apertures**, or mirrors that are used to collect and reflect light. But these apertures are

The four enormous telescopes at the Paranal Observatory in Chile together form the powerful Very Large Telescope system.

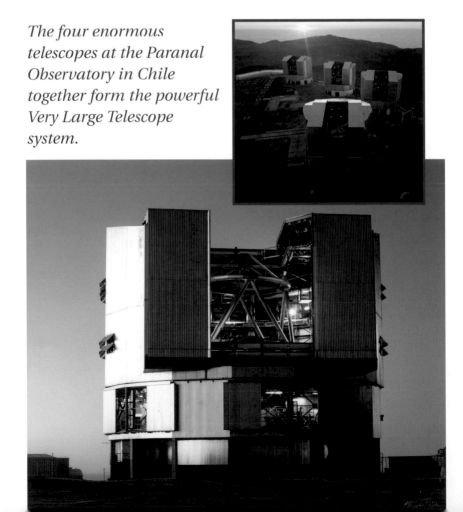

more than 30 feet (10m) across. A single piece of glass that large could not be manufactured. So, each Keck mirror is made of 36 separate pieces of glass that are fitted together much like floor tiles.

Two astronomy stations in Chile are used to observe the southern skies. They are operated by the European Southern Observatory (ESO). One, known as the Paranal Observatory, has four telescopes that are each more than 26 feet (8m) across. Together, these instruments form what is called the Very Large Telescope (VLT). Astronomy author David Darling explains how powerful the instruments are: "If there were cars on the Moon, the Very Large Telescope would be able to read their number plates."[7]

The ESO's second astronomy station, La Silla Observatory, also has high-powered telescopes. In March 2005, ESO astronomers discovered a **super star cluster** within the Milky Way. Super star clusters are groups of hundreds of thousands of baby stars packed tightly into a small area. Known as Westerlund 1, the cluster contains stars that shine with the brilliance of a million suns. Some of the stars are 2,000 times larger than Earth's sun. Astronomers have observed super star clusters in the past, but none were in Earth's own galaxy.

The Future

Scientists continue to develop instruments that are bigger and even more powerful. For example, the

This is an artist's drawing of NASA's James Webb Space Telescope, which will be used to study stars in deep space.

ESO has begun planning for a mega-telescope known as the OverWhelmingly Large Telescope, or OWL. The organization's goal is to fit together 1,600 separate mirrors to form one 328-foot (100-m) aperture. If built, the OWL would be ten times larger than any telescope in existence. It is an aggressive project, though, and one that is expected to cost more than $1 billion. Because of the great expense, as well as the work involved, the ESO estimates that OWL will not be operational until about 2020.

NASA is designing another futuristic telescope. Known as the James Webb Space Telescope (JWST), it is planned for operation in 2011. Like the Hubble, the JWST will operate from space rather than on the ground. NASA explains why another space telescope is needed: "Hubble won't last forever. . . . [It] has been in space for almost 14 years and is only expected to last another 6 years. Also the technology used on Hubble is fairly old. Hubble was built using technology from the early 1980s whereas JWST will include new state-of-the-art technology."[8] The JWST will be able to look deeper into space than any instrument ever developed because it will be so much farther out in space—1 million miles (1.6 million km) from Earth. Also, the new spacecraft will have an aperture that is six times larger than the Hubble's, as well as other sophisticated equipment.

Modern astronomers use constellations as a way of mapping the skies. Using tools that are sophisticated and powerful, they can study the stars in Earth's own galaxy as well as stars in distant galaxies. In time, this may help unlock the secrets of the universe, including how it formed and how it will continue to evolve in the future.

Chapter 1: Pictures in the Sky

1. Isaac Asimov, "Looking at the Stars," introduction to Lloyd Motz and Carol Nathanson, *The Constellations: An Enthusiast's Guide to the Night Sky*. New York: Doubleday, 1988, p. xii.
2. Chris Sasaki, *The Constellations: Stars and Stories*. New York: Sterling, 2002, p. 9.
3. H.A. Rey, *The Stars: A New Way to See Them*. Boston: Houghton Mifflin, 1980, p. 23.

Chapter 2: Mapping the Heavens

4. Von Del Chamberlain, "A Hunting We Go for Beasts That Lurk Along the Zodiac," The Clark Foundation Project Astro Utah. www.clark foundation.org/astro-utah/vondel/zodiac.html.

Chapter 3: Guided by the Stars

5. Teresa Coughlin, "Planting by the Stars," *Organic Matters,* 2002. www.organicmatters mag.com/gardening_tips/planting_by_the_stars.htm.

Chapter 4: Star Exploration

6. NASA HubbleSite Reference Desk. www.hub blesite.org/reference_desk.

7. David Darling, "Very Large Telescope (VLT)," *The Encyclopedia of Astrobiology, Astronomy, and Spaceflight.* www.daviddarling.info/ency clopedia/V/VLT.html.

8. NASA James Webb Space Telescope. http:// ngst.gsfc.nasa.gov/science/Outreach/kids.html.

apertures: Mirrors on a telescope that are used to reflect and capture light.

asterism: A star formation that is inside a constellation.

astrology: The study of how earthly events are influenced by the Sun, Moon, planets, and stars.

astronomers: Scientists who study the stars and planets.

atlas: A collection of maps.

biodynamic gardening: A gardening method that relies on the movements of the Moon, planets, and stars.

constellations: Combinations of stars that humans have arranged into imaginary patterns.

ecliptic: The invisible path that the Sun appears to travel along in the sky.

galaxies: Vast accumulations of millions or billions of stars that are held together by gravity.

geocentric system: The belief that the Earth is the center of the universe and the Sun and planets revolve around it.

horoscopes: Diagrams of the signs of the zodiac based on the positions of celestial bodies.

Hubble Space Telescope: An enormous and powerful telescope that continuously orbits the Earth.

light-years: A measure of distance used for stars that are trillions of miles or kilometers away from Earth.

Milky Way: The galaxy of which Earth and its solar system are a part.

nebulae: Giant gas and dust clouds where stars form.

spectrometers: Instruments that help astronomers estimate a star's temperature and age by examining its color.

super star cluster: A group of hundreds of thousands of very young stars.

zodiac: A family of constellations that stretches like a band across the sky.

Books

Gregory Crawford, *Animals in the Stars: Chinese Astrology for Children.* Rochester, VT: Bear Cub Books, 2003. A beautifully illustrated book about the Chinese astrological system, which teaches that people's individual character traits are influenced by celestial bodies.

Michael Driscoll, *A Child's Introduction to the Night Sky: The Story of the Stars, Planets, and Constellations—and How You Can Find Them in the Sky.* New York: Black Dog & Leventhal, 2004. An entertaining introduction to astronomy and stargazing that discusses great scientists in history, the story of the solar system, myths about constellations, and how to study the night sky.

C.E. Thompson, *Glow-in-the-Dark Constellations: A Field Guide for Young Stargazers.* New York: Grosset & Dunlap, 1999. Explains what stars are, how constellations got their names, and interesting stories associated with some of the most well-known constellations. Nice illustrations and diagrams.

Janice VanCleave, *Janice VanCleave's Constellations for Every Kid.* New York: Wiley, 1997. Features explanations of stars and constellations, as well as activities that help young people gain a better understanding of the topic.

Periodicals

Linda Carlow, "Dot-to-Dot Dippers," *Children's Digest*, March 1999.

Leisa Clark, "Constellations" *Science Weekly*, December 12, 2002.

Internet Sources

Dr. Cathy Imhoff, "Answers to Kids' Questions About the Stars," *Scholastic*. http://teacher.scholastic.com/researchtools/articlearchives/space/qastars.htm.

Web Sites

Astronomy for Kids (www.kidsastronomy.com). This excellent site features information about stars, galaxies, planets, black holes, and space exploration.

Hubblesite (www.hubblesite.org). The official Web site of the Hubble Space Telescope. Includes a beautiful collection of color photos, information about stars and planets, current news, and a special "Fun & Games" section.

NASA Kids (http://kids.msfc.nasa.gov). This fun site for kids has a good collection of facts about stars, constellations, galaxies, and the solar system.

The Science Spot Kid Zone (http://sciencespot.net/Pages/kdzastro2.html). An informative and well-designed site that covers the life cycle of stars, myths about the sky, star maps, and a constellation table.

Index

Picture Credits

About the Author

Peggy J. Parks holds a bachelor of science degree from Aquinas College in Grand Rapids, Michigan, where she graduated magna cum laude. An avid fan of all things related to earth science and astronomy, Parks has written more than 40 titles for Thomson Gale's KidHaven Press, Blackbirch Press, and Lucent Books imprints. She lives in Muskegon, Michigan, a town she says inspires her writing because of its location on the shores of Lake Michigan.